HAL•LEONARD

INSTRUMENTAL PLAY-ALONG

VIOLA

AUDIO ACCESS INCLUDED

PLAYBACK+
Speed • Pitch • Balance • Loop

Disney · PIXAR
COCO

T0070794

2   Everyone Knows Juanita

4   La Llorona

3   Much Needed Advice

6   Proud Corazón

7   Remember Me (Ernesto de la Cruz)

8   Un Poco Loco

10 The World Es Mi Familia

Audio arrangements by Peter Deneff

To access audio visit:
www.halleonard.com/mylibrary

Enter Code
2726-1306-1695-0336

ISBN 978-1-5400-2141-0

HAL•LEONARD®

7777 W. BLUEMOUND RD. P.O. BOX 13819 MILWAUKEE, WI 53213

In Australia Contact:
Hal Leonard Australia Pty. Ltd.
4 Lentara Court
Cheltenham, Victoria, 3192 Australia
Email: ausadmin@halleonard.com.au

Visit Hal Leonard Online at
www.halleonard.com

EVERYONE KNOWS JUANITA
from COCO

VIOLA

Music by GERMAINE FRANCO
Lyrics by ADRIAN MOLINA

MUCH NEEDED ADVICE
from COCO

VIOLA

Music by MICHAEL GIACCHINO
and GERMAINE FRANCO
Lyrics by ADRIAN MOLINA

LA LLORONA
from COCO

VIOLA

Traditional Mexican Folksong
Arranged by GERMAINE FRANCO

PROUD CORAZÓN
from COCO

VIOLA

Music by GERMAINE FRANCO
Lyrics by ADRIAN MOLINA

REMEMBER ME

(Ernesto de la Cruz)

from COCO

VIOLA

Words and Music by KRISTEN ANDERSON-LOPEZ
and ROBERT LOPEZ

UN POCO LOCO

from COCO

Music by GERMAINE FRANCO
Lyrics by ADRIAN MOLINA

VIOLA

THE WORLD ES MI FAMILIA

from COCO

VIOLA

Music by GERMAINE FRANCO
Lyrics by ADRIAN MOLINA